❶ The stitch cards are numbered 1–60 and **color-coded** by stitch category to make it easy to find the card you need.

❷ **Stitch Number** is top left on the card and is included in the index.

❸ **L/R** next to the stitch number denotes the left- or right-handed stitch side.

❹ **Stitch category** is listed on the top right of the card.

❺ **A photo** of the single stitch is toward the top of the card.

❻ The main part of the card features the **how-to instructions**.

❼ **Repeated illustrations** along the bottom of the card show what the stitch would look like along a seamline.

Threads, Floss & Needles

THREADS AND FLOSS

Floss is a flat six-stranded thread that comes wrapped in a skein, or three-strands wound on a spool. A variety of fiber contents are available, including cotton, linen, silk, and rayon. Cotton and silk can be found in solid, ombré, variegated, and hand-dyed colors. Linen and rayon floss can be found in solid colors.

Perle cotton is a two-ply twisted cotton thread that gives stitches some dimension and comes in a skein or a ball; it is available in a variety of solid, ombré, variegated, and hand-dyed colors.

1. Perle cotton #5, #8, and #12
2. Hand-dyed perle cotton
3. Stranded floss: cotton, silk, linen, and rayon

Contents

HOW TO USE THE CARD SET 2

THREADS, FLOSS & NEEDLES 4

Threads and Floss 4

Needles 5

EMBROIDERY BASICS 6

Tips for Threading the Needle 6

Knots 6

Stitch Direction 7

Stitch Length 7

Adding Thread 8

STITCH INDEX 9

ABOUT THE AUTHOR 16

How to Use the Card Set

Welcome to your *On-the-Go Embroidery Cards Set 1*! Designed as a fun, flexible, and portable way to bring your embroidery stitch instructions along with you, it includes 60 stitch cards, three floss organizers, three metal project rings, and this instruction booklet featuring embroidery basics (pages 6–8) and a visual index (pages 9–15).

Load the floss you love and grab the stitch cards you need. Put them on a project ring and off you go! Take your embroidery on your next adventure.

NEEDLES

The purpose of the needle is to make a hole in the fabric big enough for the thread to pass through the fabric, but not so big that it will damage the fabric. As a general rule, the shaft of the needle should be the same thickness as the thread. Needles are sized from low to high; the lower the number, the larger the needle.

1. Cotton darner: a long needle with an oval eye that is used for twisted threads

2. Crewel (also called embroidery needles): a long needle with a long to medium eye that is wider than the shaft; used for twisted threads

3. Embroidery: a fine, thin needle with a long eye that is used for stranded floss

Embroidery Basics

TIPS FOR THREADING THE NEEDLE

- Always cut the end of the thread straight across the grain.
- Pinch and/or wet the tip of the thread.
- Wet the eye of the needle; the moisture will attract the thread.
- Use a needle threader for floss or perle cotton.
- Try a magnifier glass with a light source.
- Hire a teenager who has great eyesight to thread your needles. (Don't laugh; I used to do this for a dear friend of mine!)

KNOTS

Once the needle is threaded, I knot the tail. After I work a row of stitches, I knot the thread on the wrong side and cut the thread. I then make a knot in the remaining thread, ready for the next row of stitches.

Or instead, you could tack the thread at the beginning and end of a row. Make a tack stitch into the foundation of muslin or interfacing (not through the top layer). Take another tack stitch next to the first, pulling the thread to make a loop. Insert the needle through the loop and pull the knot closed.

STITCH DIRECTION

Keep the direction of your stitches in mind. The direction in which the stitch should be worked is based on the design. For instance, the chain stitch can be worked in any direction out from a design, but the feather stitch is started away from a design and worked toward it.

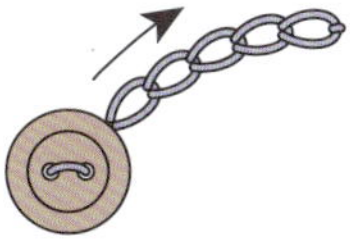

Chain stitch worked out of a vignette

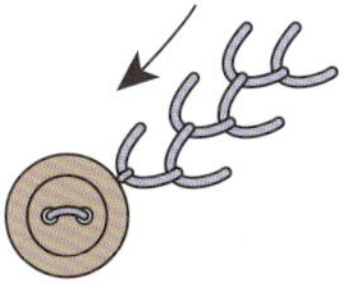

Feather stitch worked into a vignette

STITCH LENGTH

The stitch length should directly correlate to the size of the thread you are using. In general, take a smaller stitch when using a fine thread or fewer strands of floss; take a larger stitch for heavier threads or for more strands of floss.

Variations in Length

Changing the distance between **A**, **B**, and **C** can vary the shape of the stitch. (Fly stitch shown below.)

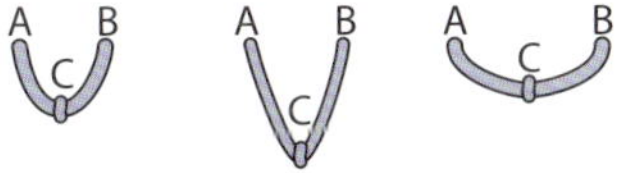

At the left, the spacing between **A**, **B**, and **C** is equal. At the center, **A** and **B** are closer, and **C** is farther apart. At the right, **A** and **B** are farther apart, and **C** is closer.

ADDING THREAD

Straight Stitches: Backstitch or Outline, Stem, Heringbone, or Chevron Stitch

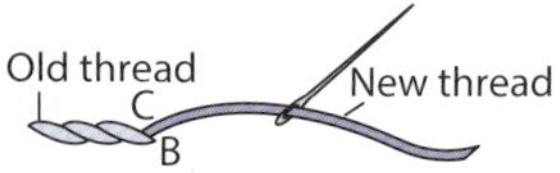

Knot and cut the old thread after **B**; start the new thread at **C**.

Looped Stitches: Feather, Blanket, Buttonhole, Cretan, or Chain Stitch

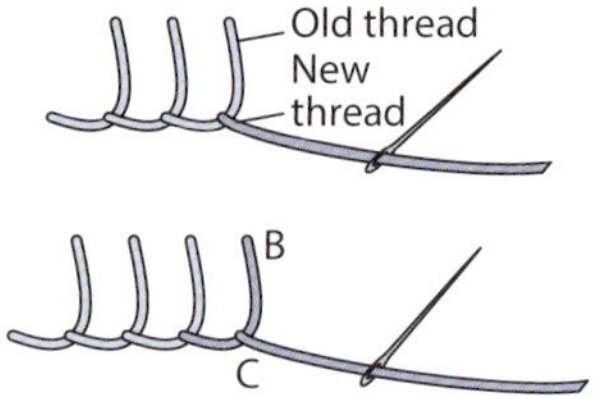

1. Stitch **B** of a looped stitch down through the fabric, but do not pull the thread taut. Stitch a new thread through the loop at **C**. Pull the old thread to form the loop.

2. Stitch 1 or 2 stitches with the new thread; then knot and cut the old thread. Continue to stitch with the new thread.

Stitch Index

01 · STRAIGHT STITCH

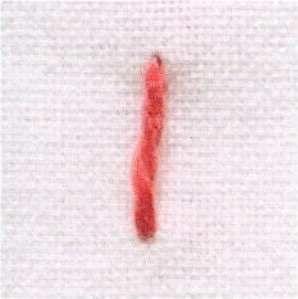

02 · PISTIL STITCH

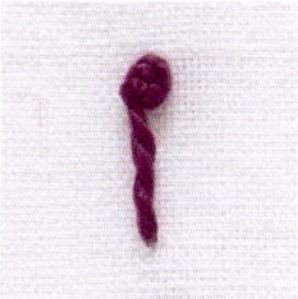

03 · FIVE-POINT STAR STITCH

04 · STRAIGHT-STITCH FLOWERS

05 · WHEAT EAR STITCH MODIFIED

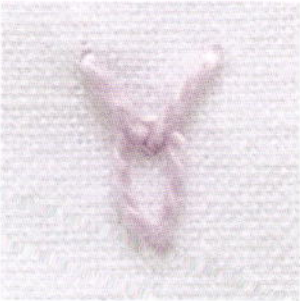

06 · OUTLINE STITCH

07 · STEM STITCH

08 · STEM/OUTLINE FERN STITCH

09 · BACKSTITCH

10 · LAZY DAISY STITCH

11 · LOOPED TENDRIL STITCH

12 · LAZY DAISY STITCH FLOWERS

13 · LAZY DAISY HEART STITCH

14 · LAZY DAISY TULIP STITCH

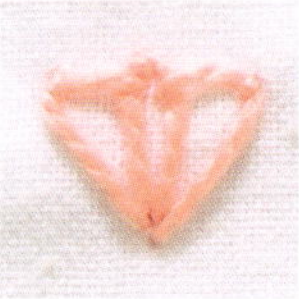

15 · CHAIN STITCH

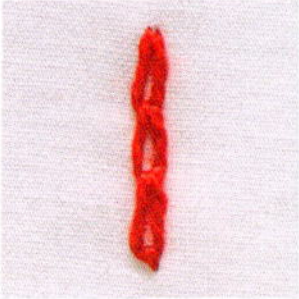

16 · CHAIN STITCH ZIG ZAG

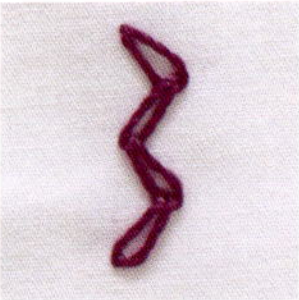

17 · CHAIN STITCH FEATHERED

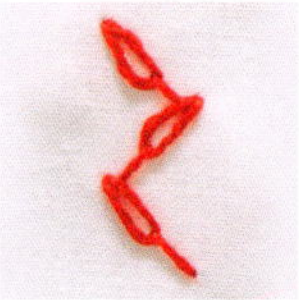

18 · CHAIN STITCH DOUBLE

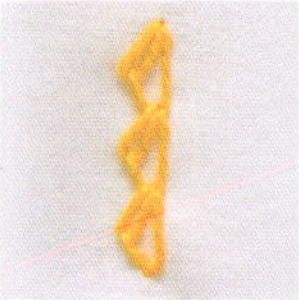

19 · BARB STITCH

20 · BARB STITCH LOOPED

21 · CROSSED WIRE STITCH

22 · SANTA FE STAR STITCH

23 · BARB STITCH WITH KNOT TIP

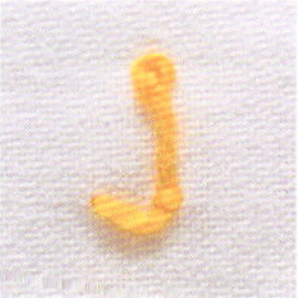

24 · BLANKET STITCH

25 · BLANKET STITCH CLOSED

26 · BLANKET STITCH UP AND DOWN

27 · LEAVES AND STEM STALK OR ROW

28 · BELL FLOWER STITCH

29 · CROSSED TRIANGLE STITCH

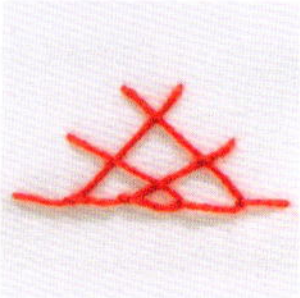

30 · SUNRISE STITCH

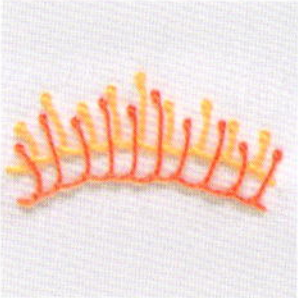

31 · BUTTONHOLE CIRCLE STITCH

32 · FRENCH KNOT

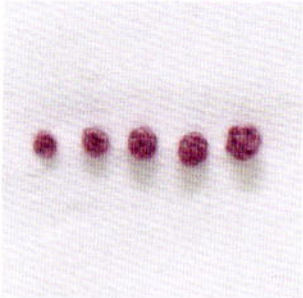

33 · FRENCH KNOT STITCH FLOWERS

34 · BARNACLE STITCH

35 · FLY STITCH

36 · FISHHOOK STITCH

37 · FERN STITCH MODERN

38 · FLY STITCH FLOWERS

39 · FEATHER STITCH

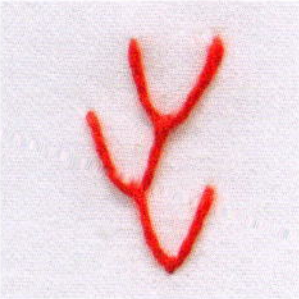

40 · FEATHER STITCH DOUBLE

41 · FEATHER STITCH PIGGYBACK

42 · FISHNET STITCH

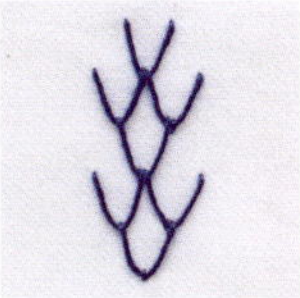

43 · FEATHER STITCH TWISTED

44 · FLEET STITCH

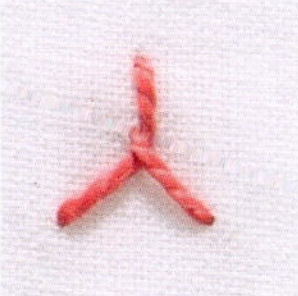

45 · FLEET STITCH LOOPED

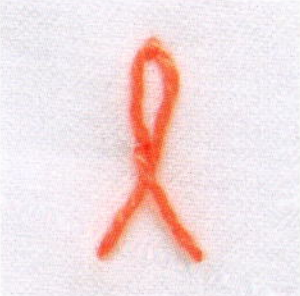

46 · FLEET STITCH WITH KNOT TIP

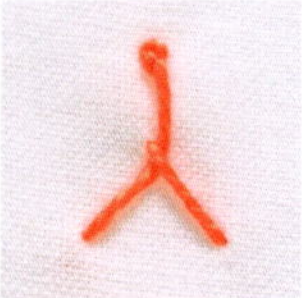

47 · STEEPLE AND CROSS STITCH

48 · FLEET STITCH FLOWERS

49 · CRETAN STITCH 4-ROW

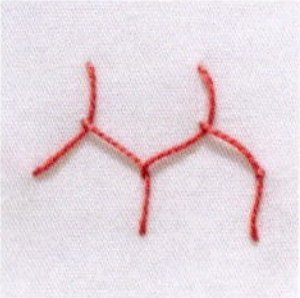

50 · CRETAN STITCH WITH LOOSE KNOT

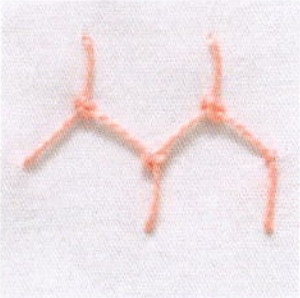

51 · CRETAN STITCH WITH SPRIG TIP

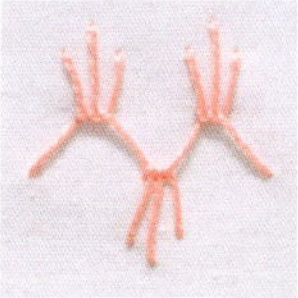

52 · CROSS STITCH

53 · CROSS STITCH ROW

54 · FOUR CORNER CROSS STITCH

55 · HERRINGBONE STITCH

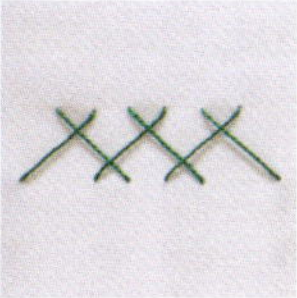

56 · HERRINGBONE AND CROSS STITCH SINGLE

57 · HERRINGBONE STITCH BOXED

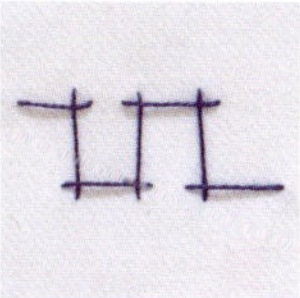

58 · CHEVRON STITCH

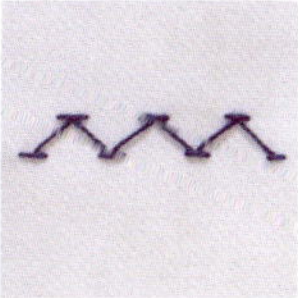

59 · CHEVRON STITCH M-W

60 · SAWTOOTH STITCH

About the Author

Christen Brown teaches embroidery, quilting, ribbonwork, mixed media, and beadwork in her best-selling books. With a degree in fashion design, she has shown her work in galleries and fashion shows all over the world. She lives in Escondido, California. Visit Christen on the web at **christenbrown.com**